Too Cute!
Baby Monkeys

by Rachael Barnes

Blastoff! Beginners

BELLWETHER MEDIA
MINNEAPOLIS, MN

Blastoff! Beginners are developed by literacy experts and educators to meet the needs of early readers. These engaging informational texts support young children as they begin reading about their world. Through simple language and high frequency words paired with crisp, colorful photos, Blastoff! Beginners launch young readers into the universe of independent reading.

Sight Words in This Book 🔍

and	from	on	the
are	get	other	their
at	help	play	they
big	her	ride	up
eat	in	she	with
find	look	soon	

This edition first published in 2023 by Bellwether Media, Inc.

No part of this publication may be reproduced in whole or in part without written permission of the publisher. For information regarding permission, write to Bellwether Media, Inc., Attention: Permissions Department, 6012 Blue Circle Drive, Minnetonka, MN 55343.

Library of Congress Cataloging-in-Publication Data

Names: Barnes, Rachael, author.
Title: Baby monkeys / by Rachael Barnes.
Description: Minneapolis, MN : Bellwether Media, 2023. | Series: Blastoff! beginners: Too cute! | Includes bibliographical references and index. | Audience: Ages 4-7 | Audience: Grades K-1
Identifiers: LCCN 2022012993 (print) | LCCN 2022012994 (ebook) | ISBN 9781644876701 (library binding) | ISBN 9781648347160 (ebook)
Subjects: LCSH: Monkeys--Infancy--Juvenile literature. Classification: LCC QL737.P925 B37 2023 (print) | LCC QL737.P925 (ebook) | DDC 599.813/92--dc23/eng/20220329
LC record available at https://lccn.loc.gov/2022012993
LC ebook record available at https://lccn.loc.gov/2022012994

Text copyright © 2023 by Bellwether Media, Inc. BLASTOFF! BEGINNERS and associated logos are trademarks and/or registered trademarks of Bellwether Media, Inc.

Editor: Christina Leaf   Designer: Jeffrey Kollock

Printed in the United States of America, North Mankato, MN.

Table of Contents

A Baby Monkey!	4
Life in the Trees	6
Growing Up	18
Baby Monkey Facts	22
Glossary	23
To Learn More	24
Index	24

A Baby Monkey!

Look at the baby monkey. Hello, infant!

infant

Life in the Trees

Infants live in trees. They live with their families.

Infants ride on mom. They hold on tight!

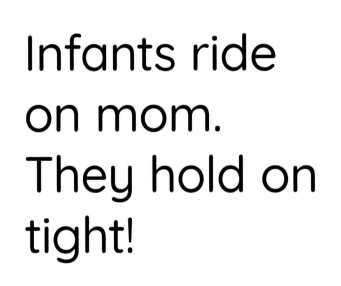

They **nurse**.
They drink milk from mom.

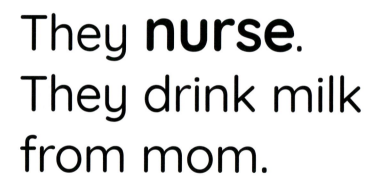

Mom helps older infants find food. They eat plants and bugs.

Mom **grooms** her infant. She cleans its fur.

Infants play with other babies. They **wrestle**!

wrestling

Growing Up

Infants get stronger. They **swing** from trees!

swinging

Infants get big.
They learn fast.
Soon they are
grown up!

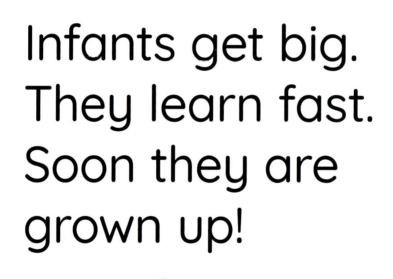

Baby Monkey Facts

Monkey Life Stages

infant   young monkey   adult

A Day in the Life

ride on mom

be groomed by mom

wrestle

22

Glossary

grooms

cleans

nurse

to drink mom's milk

swing

to move back and forth while holding on

wrestle

to fight by holding and pushing

To Learn More

ON THE WEB

FACTSURFER

Factsurfer.com gives you a safe, fun way to find more information.

1. Go to www.factsurfer.com.

2. Enter "baby monkeys" into the search box and click 🔍.

3. Select your book cover to see a list of related content.

Index

big, 20
bugs, 12
cleans, 14
drink, 10
eat, 12
families, 6
find, 12
food, 12
fur, 14

grooms, 14, 15
helps, 12
hold, 8
learn, 20
milk, 10
mom, 8, 10, 12, 14
monkey, 4
nurse, 10, 11

plants, 12
play, 16
ride, 8
swing, 18, 19
trees, 6, 18
wrestle, 16, 17

The images in this book are reproduced through the courtesy of: wizdata1, front cover; Eric Isselee, pp. 3, 4, 5, 20, 22 (young, adult); achikochi, pp. 6-7; Michal Ninger, pp. 8-9; Anders Riishede, p. 10; Svetlana Orusova, pp. 10-11; trubavin, pp. 12-13; Sharon Haeger, pp. 14-15; David Bokuchava, pp. 16-17; Sompao, pp. 18-19, 20-21, 23 (swing); bludog studio, p. 22 (newborn); Jess Kraft, p. 22 (ride); LNLong, p. 22 (groomed); Andreas Altenburger, p. 22 (wrestle); WD Stock Photos, p. 23 (grooms); OlegD, p. 23 (nurse); MyImages - Micha, p. 23 (wrestle).